CURTIS INTERNATIONAL
PORTRAITS OF GREATNESS

•

General Editor
Enzo Orlandi

Text by
Alfredo Panicucci

Translator
C. J. Richards

Published by
ARNOLDO MONDADORI EDITORE
and
THE CURTIS PUBLISHING COMPANY

THE LIFE & TIMES OF LOUIS XIV

A division of
The Curtis Publishing Company
Philadelphia • New York

A GIFT FROM GOD

The birth of the future Louis XIV was a grand affair of state. It was also an event that fell just short of being miraculous, for the King and Queen had been married for 23 years and they detested each other. After all these years of unfruitful marriage, everyone had become resigned to the idea that the reigning couple, Louis XIII and Anne of Austria, would remain childless. This meant the King's brother, Gaston d'Orléans, would eventually inherit the throne. But, on September 5, 1638, amid national rejoicing (though not Gaston's), the birth of an heir to the throne was proclaimed with bells, trumpets and cannons. France finally had her longed-for "Dauphin," as the heir to the French throne has been called since the acquisition by France, in 1349, of the province of Dauphiné. It was a miracle, said the Queen. Truly a miracle, sighed the sickly Louis XIII. The chubby baby, who was said to have a ravenous appetite, was given the name of "Dieudonné"—the gift of God—in addition to the ancestral one of Louis. He really was a gift from Heaven.

Anne of Austria, daughter of the King of Spain, Philip III, had married Louis XIII in 1615. With this sumptuous royal wedding, which had taken place in Bordeaux, France and Spain promised one another peace. The bride and groom were each 14. As the years passed, however, it became apparent that Louis had little interest in his Spanish bride, and often went without seeing her for months at a time. The Queen could already see herself, widowed and childless, sent back to Spain to some gloomy convent. If there was to be a convent, better to be in a cheerful French one. Accordingly, Anne spent a great deal of time visiting these and praying for a son. Finally, the miracle occurred and the shadow of a Spanish convent vanished. In thanksgiving, Anne of Austria made a vow, which she kept, to build a church at Val-de-Grâce. It was to have a cupola 40 meters high so that it could be seen for miles.

Left: The Church of Val-de-Grâce, from a drawing by Le Clerc. Louis XIV, in response to his mother's vow, laid the cornerstone, April 1, 1645. The cupola, designed by Gabriel Le Duc, reflects the influence of Michelangelo. Below, opposite page: Philippe de Champaigne's painting of Louis XIII being crowned by Victory. Below, left: Mignard's painting of Anne of Austria. Below, right: Gaston d'Orléans, brother of Louis XIII, from a portrait by Van Dyck. He spent his life plotting first against his brother, then against his royal nephew. It was said of him that "he entered into the conspiracies because of lack of will, and he always crept shamefully out of them because of lack of courage." Nonetheless, at the death of Louis XIII, he was appointed Lieutenant-General of the kingdom in accordance with his brother's wishes.

THE LEGACY OF RICHELIEU

Above and below: The vanquished commanders of the battle of Rocroi: Don Francisco de Mello, Governor of the Low Countries and Commander-in-Chief of the Spanish forces; Don Pedro Enriquez de Acevedo, Count of Fuentes, who died on the field, leading his infantry. Right: Heim's painting of the battle. The Duc D'Enghien is shown trying to halt his cavalry. It was in the process of turning the victory into a massacre because the Spaniards, after surrendering, had misunderstood a movement of the French and reopened fire on them.

On May 13, 1643, as Louis XIII lay dying of tuberculosis, his eyes came to rest on the Prince de Condé, and he said to him: "Monsieur, I know that the enemy has penetrated our territory with a large and powerful army, but your son will throw back its advance and quiet our anxiety." No one paid attention to the delirium of a dying man. The next day, Louis XIII died. But his prophecy had come true. Five days later the 22-year-old Duc d'Enghien, the son of the Prince de Condé, defeated the Spanish forces under the command of Francisco de Mello. The battle took place at Rocroi, a small village in the Ardennes, two miles from the present-day Belgian border. The army upon which depended the fate of France was part of the legacy of Louis XIII's great minister, Cardinal de Richelieu, who had died a few months before his king, on December 4, 1642. One of the most valuable parts of this legacy was an infantry of 150,000 men and a cavalry of 30,000. Richelieu, as prime minister, had laid the foundations of absolute monarchy. He had reduced the strength and the prestige of the great nobles and broken the power of the Huguenots. He had succeeded in separating politics from religion in both domestic and foreign affairs. The result of all this had been a vigorous centralization of power, which Louis XIV was to exploit to the utmost. Last of all, he had entrusted the continuity of his work to a loyal successor, the devoted and able Mazarin. But there were shadows in this picture. Military expenses in the last 10 years had more than doubled, a serious strain on the economy. The Thirty Years' War, with its military and political complications, was not yet finished, even if the decisive French victory at Rocroi bore the promise of a final solution. However, peace finally did come five years later with the Treaties of Westphalia in 1648. By these treaties France obtained, among other things, the cities and bishoprics of Metz, Toul and Verdun, former Austrian possessions in Alsace. The strength and influence of the House of Hapsburg were reduced, the Holy Roman Empire began to disintegrate, and separate German states to emerge. France was now firmly planted on the Rhine and in a position to interfere in German affairs. Richelieu, from the great beyond, could take pride in his accomplishments and in that of his successor.

THE KING IS DEAD—LONG LIVE THE KING

Below and right: Three moments in the battle of Rocroi as painted by Alphonse Lalauze. Directly below: Condé's aide, General Gassion, patrolling the woods near Rocroi on the eve of the decisive encounter. Opposite page: 1) the lame veteran, Count of Fuentes, being carried on the battlefield to observe his crack Spanish infantry repulse the French. 2) The Duc D'Enghien inspecting his forces before the attack. It was only with their third charge that the French were finally able to overcome the dogged resistance of the Spaniards. Outstanding among these was the famous Tercio, the best infantry in the world at that time.

The victory of Rocroi was a good omen for the new king, who was barely five years old. He needed good omens. His reign, which was later to shine so brightly, opened amid many shadows. The first of these was the will left by Louis XIII, who distrusted both his wife and his cowardly and treacherous brother, the Duc d'Orléans. Under the terms of the will, his widow, Anne of Austria, was appointed Regent and his brother, Lieutenant-General of the kingdom. As a safeguard, a council of four was set up without whose consent the Queen was powerless to act. These councillors were Condé (the father of the brilliant young victor of Rocroi), Mazarin, and two of Richelieu's trusted men. The Regency Council was an ill-assorted one. Gaston d'Orléans was not kindly disposed toward his nephew, whose birth had put the throne out of his reach. Condé, a Bourbon prince, had royal ambitions himself. He did not get along with the Queen Mother nor with his cousin, the Duc d'Orléans. As for the other members of the council, he considered them beneath his notice.

Anne of Austria had not had an easy life. Her husband detested her, and she had nothing but scorn for him. She had, throughout, borne herself with quiet dignity. However, the final affront, having her power as Regent curtailed by her husband's last-minute will, did nothing to salve her pride. She determined to exert some authority at last. For once, she and the Duc d'Orléans were in agreement on one point: the necessity for the annulment of the late King's testament. Their efforts were seconded by Mazarin, the only member of the council who had any notion of what was required for a stable and effective government. He knew perfectly well that if the Regency Council were allowed to stand, all that Richelieu had accomplished in strengthening and centralizing the royal power would be wiped out. Condé lent his support because, as a prince of the blood, he considered it humiliating to have the powers of a member of the royal family, even of one he disliked, curtailed by a lesser breed of mortals. The remaining two men in the council fell in with the plan because they hoped to ingratiate themselves with the Regent. It did not take them long to discover they had miscalculated.

Left: Parade by the Swiss guards carrying banners, pennons and other flags taken from the Spaniards at the battle of Rocroi. They are on their way to Notre-Dame for the Te Deum of May 26, 1643, celebrating the victory. Queen Anne and her son watched the parade from a window of the Louvre.

THE BREAKING OF THE WILL

Directly below: Portrait of the infant Louis XIV with his mother, Anne of Austria, by an artist of the school of 17th-century French painting. Bottom of page: Louis XIV being presented to the Parlement *of Paris, from a contemporary print. According to the caption, written in verse, the* Parlement *accepts Anne as Regent and praises the Queen and the King, terming them "adorable." Right: Portrait of the 10-year-old Louis XIV, by Henri Testelin (1616-1695). Paintings of Louis XIV are countless. For almost a century he was admired and exalted by generations of artists, painters, sculptors, engravers and decorators.*

In order to put the Queen's plan into action—that is, the breaking of the King's will—the cooperation of the Paris *Parlement* was required. This body was essentially a court of judges. Its powers, never extensive, had been further diminished by the repressive measures taken by both Louis XIII and by Richelieu. However, its support would be invaluable to Anne of Austria in asserting her authority over the great nobles, who had lost no time in showing an alarming independence. Accordingly, on the morning of May 18, 1643, the Queen Mother took her son to the Palais de Justice to present him to *Parlement*. The youngster gazed calmly at the assembled scarlet-robed magistrates, and spoke in a clear, steady treble the sentence he had learned: "Gentlemen, I have come to see you in order to express my affection and goodwill toward my *Parlement*. My Chancellor will tell you my will." Louis' will, of course, was his mother's. The *Parlement*, which, like Anne, had suffered under Richelieu's iron hand, declared that the "royal authority should be one and indivisible," and voted to abolish the Regency Council. It was announced further that the King was pleased to give his mother "free, absolute and entire administration of the affairs of his kingdom during his minority." In this way Anne finally obtained the power she considered hers by right. However, her talents were not up to the responsibility, and she had the sense, most of the time, to realize it. She was inclined to be lazy and emotional. She knew nothing of taxes or bribery. She was too straightforward and simple-minded to deal with the plots her courtiers were constantly hatching. A man was needed to govern France. The late King's brother had neither the intelligence nor the courage to deal with affairs of state. The Prince de Condé was too self-seeking. Once again Mazarin came to the fore. He was an attractive, well-dressed young man who, although self-effacing, always managed to be on hand when advice was needed. The Queen Regent made him prime minister. She also appointed him Superintendent of the Education of the King. His authority over Louis XIV was unquestioned, and the rules of government Louis learned from him proved later to be invaluable: the necessity for personal government, distrust of the great nobles, the sound management of finances, and the necessity for justice.

A REBELLIOUS PARLEMENT

The Paris *Parlement* had counted on ingratiating itself with her. It came as a shock and a surprise to discover that the Queen had no further use for it. Ever since Richelieu's death this body had been looking for a chance to assert itself, to share some authority in the government of France. Each magistrate in the *Parlement* had either paid for his office or inherited it. Among them were some whose honesty, legal knowledge and independence of mind made them an asset, but most of the members thought only of cashing in on the offices they or their forebears had paid for.

Taking advantage of the instability of the new regime and capitalizing on popular discontent, the *Parlement* declared that in the future any taxation must have its approval, and that no subject could be detained for more than 24 hours without due process of law. The Queen was furious, but she tearfully submitted, yielding to Mazarin's entreaties—he knew that she was in no position to defend the royal prerogatives because Condé and his armies were at the front. As soon as Condé had returned victorious, the Queen could deal with her enemies. However, Anne acted too soon, and against Cardinal Mazarin's advice, she ordered the arrest of three troublemakers in *Parlement*, the most prominent and popular of whom was Pierre Broussel, a 70-year-old magistrate. As soon as they had learned that this "Father of the People" had been arrested, Parisians shut up shop and marched to the royal residence, shouting "Broussel! Freedom!" Stones were flung at the royal guard, hence the name *Fronde* (slingshot), by which the civil war came to be known. The cautious, compromising Mazarin persuaded the Queen to yield. Humiliation followed humiliation for Anne and Louis XIV. Mazarin was outlawed by the *Parlement*, and the King and his small loyal following lived in destitution in Saint-Germain. There often was not enough food, the bedding was torn and insufficiently warm, and Louis' clothes were too small for him. He never forgot, nor forgave, his treatment by the people of Paris. Meantime, some of the great noble families of France joined the rebellion—the Dukes of Longueville and Beaufort, even the Prince de Conti, Condé's brother. However, Condé, the "victor of Rocroi," intervened. He was too aristocratic not to turn up his nose at the collusion between the nobles on the one hand and the magistrates and the mob on the other. With his forces he brought the rebels to heel. But Anne had to pay dearly.

Left: Three leaders of the Rebellion: Pierre Broussel, Omer Talon (both members of the Paris Parlement) *and Paul de Gondi, who later became Cardinal de Retz, a writer and spokesman for the opposition. He was exiled and spent some years in Rome. He was a scoundrel, but an articulate one: his* Memoirs, *published after the death of Louis XIV, are among the classics of French literature. Lower left: A contemporary print showing the troubles of Paris. These were the subject of a satire written in 1660 by Boileau, another of France's great writers. Two lines from it point out that even the darkest, most solitary forest is a safer place than Paris. Below left: Anne of Austria with her two sons. Below right: A gathering in Paris at the time of the* Fronde. *Bottom of the page: Painting by Antoine Durant showing a delegation of notables of the city of Toulouse paying homage to Louis XIV upon the occasion of his first visit there on October 14, 1659.*

NOBLES AGAINST THE KING

The paintings on these two pages, by Sauveur Le Conte (1659–1694), show episodes in the blockade of Paris in 1649 during the Fronde. *The great Condé led the attack against the rebellious city. Below left: The battle of Brie-Comte-Robert. Upper right: The attack against Charenton. Lower right: The battle of Vitry. Center right: Portrait of Louis II, Prince de Condé (1621–1686), known as the Great Condé. The painting was done by Juste d'Egmont when the Prince was 35. He was inordinately ambitious, and although he was at first loyal to the Crown, he later joined the rebels. Later still he allied himself with Spain against France. He was readmitted to France in 1659 and fought brilliantly in the war against the Netherlands. Bossuet's funeral oration about the Prince is a masterpiece of its kind.*

It was thanks to the Great Condé that Louis XIV, his mother and Mazarin were able to make a triumphant entry back into Paris in August of 1649. Condé, proud and arrogant, continued to exact a high price for his services. He demanded, and for a while received, all kinds of royal prerogatives, but he had reckoned without Mazarin, whom he despised as a low-born menial. The Cardinal, eternally smiling and outwardly respectful, could be as bold as the Prince. Judging Condé to have become a threat to the government, Mazarin calmly and unexpectedly (some thought treacherously) had Condé, Conti (his younger brother) and Longueville (his brother-in-law) rounded up and imprisoned. Turenne (France's other great general), who had been lured to the Rebels' side by the Duchesse de Longueville, left his command in the Low Countries and marched on Paris. Mazarin led a small force against him, and defeated him. Meantime, in Paris, Cardinal de Retz persuaded the *Parlement* to exile Mazarin. The latter prudently withdrew to a German border town, having first ordered the release of the princes. Condé then overreached himself: he allied himself with Spain, sent envoys to Cromwell in England, and promised to turn France into a republic. The situation was best summed up by that old gossip, de Retz: "We were ready, ten times a day, to slit each other's throats." From then on people changed sides continuously.

On September 8, 1651, Louis XIV, aged 13, having attained his majority, declared his mother's regency at an end and confirmed Mazarin's exile. However, he recalled him within two months. Condé, faced with Mazarin's return, marched against Paris. There he met Turenne, who had once more switched to the other side. At this point, Anne-Marie d'Orléans, daughter of Gaston d' Orléans, appeared on the scene. Despite her desire to marry the King, she was foolish enough to persuade the Governor of the Bastille to fire a few cannonades against Turenne and to open the gates of Paris to Condé. Having taken over the city, Prince de Condé found himself faced with anarchy. The nobles began to ask themselves if the authority of the King was not less dangerous than that of an exasperated populace. Mazarin, anxious to re-establish peace, returned once more into exile. On October 21, 1652, Louis XIV re-entered his capital. Condé fled to Bordeaux, the Duchesse de Longueville retired into a convent at Port-Royal and the impetuous Anne-Marie was banished to one of her estates. On February 6, 1653, when the King felt himself securely back in the saddle, he recalled the trusted Mazarin. The second *Fronde* had come to an end.

Two ladies who played an important part in the events of the Fronde: *Directly below: The King's cousin, Anne-Marie-Louise d'Orléans, Duchesse de Montpensier, known as the Grande Mademoiselle (1627-1693). Bottom of page: Condé's sister, Anne, Duchesse de Longueville (1619-1679), one of Mazarin's many sworn enemies.*

MAZARIN

Left: Portrait of Cardinal Mazarin by Pierre Mignard (1612-1695), who succeeded Le Brun as Court painter. Below: Plan of Casale during the Siege of 1630. It was here, during the morning of October 26, that the Papal Envoy, the Abbé Mazarin, rode between the French and Imperial troops to put a stop to hostilities.

Jules Mazarin may well have been France's most unpopular prime minister—at least during his lifetime. However, the perspective of history has in some measure rehabilitated his name. He was born Giulio Mazarino, the son of a Sicilian servant to the house of Colonna. An intelligent, enterprising boy, he managed to acquire, first, a top-notch university education and, second, sufficient military training to enable him to lead a papal regiment when he was in his early twenties. He then went into diplomacy, where he gave immediate proof of his talents by putting a stop to the war of the Mantuan succession between the Spaniards and the French. Later, when he had been appointed papal nuncio to Paris, he was noticed and chosen by Richelieu to join his staff. Upon the death of Louis XIII, Anne of Austria, who was looking for a trustworthy minister as unlike Richelieu as possible, found the smiling, ingratiating, but shrewd Cardinal Mazarin always available, always ready with workable solutions to even the knottiest problems. Mazarin's undoubted talents showed up most clearly in his foreign policy, which was merely a continuation of Richelieu's: the humbling of the House of Austria, the extension of France's frontiers to the Rhine, the counter-balancing of German states against Austria, the successful conclusion of the Thirty Years' War. All these aims were achieved by the Peace of Westphalia.

Mazarin's domestic policy was less successful. The disorders of the *Fronde* occurred in large part because of his insensitivity to French reactions. He was hated by everyone—by the nobles because he reduced even further what power was left them; by the bourgeois, who feared for their hereditary offices; by the common people because he was not French. And all classes resented his avarice, his plundering of the treasury, his lavish way of life, his dandified appearance.

He had amassed a huge personal fortune out of public funds. His favorite method was the sale of government posts. For example, a counselor to *Parlement* had to pay 100,000 *livres* for the privilege; a chairman, 350,000 *livres*. But if Mazarin helped himself generously to public funds, he also knew how to spend. He disbursed 300,000 *livres* to buy the cooperation of certain members of *Parlement*. He saw to it that government salaries were paid regularly. He spent money liberally on institutions and foundations that did France honor, and he set up a system of pensioning for artists and men of letters.

The Queen's affection and loyalty to him never wavered. Gossips claimed that she and the Cardinal were secretly married (he had never been ordained a priest), but there is no evidence to support the allegation. Louis XIV had a deep respect and admiration for him, and apparently never resented the close bond between his mother and his prime minister. Mazarin may have failed, as has often been charged, as a schoolmaster (Louis XIV was extraordinarily unlearned), but as a guide and teacher for a young king he was eminently successful. He instilled in Louis the basic rules for government and diplomacy. His final advice to his royal pupil was: "Sire, . . . never have a Prime Minister. . . . Govern! Let the politician be a servant, never a master. . . . If you take the government into your own hands, you will do more in one day than a minister cleverer than I in six months." Louis never forgot the advice. Mazarin died at Vincennes on March 9, 1661. There was general rejoicing at the news, and his doctor, Guenot, was hailed warmly and enthusiastically as the man who had hastened his death. Mazarin left, in tangible possessions, a huge fortune, a magnificent art collection and a superb library that is still the joy of scholars. But his greatest legacy was an intangible one—a nation at peace, a stable, centralized government and a staff of well-trained administrators. Cardinal Mazarin had sent for some of his sister's

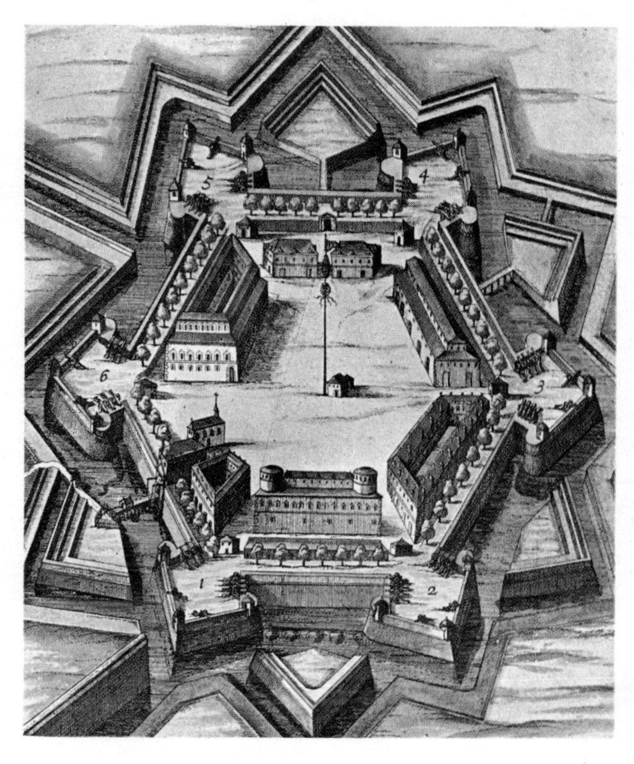

children to come live in Paris with him: Laure, Olympe, Hortense, Marie, Anne and Marie-Anne, the "Mazarinettes" as they were called. They were married off to some of the oldest and noblest families of France and Italy. Olympe, for example, married the Count of Savoie-Soissons and later became the mother of the famous Prince Eugène. Had Mazarin been the unscrupulous schemer he was reported to be, he could have made Marie the queen of France. Frequently a visitor to the Cardinal's house, where he came into contact with a world of culture and elegance, young Louis XIV had fallen in love with the youngest Mancini girl. Marie, who apparently was a born schemer, already saw herself crowned. But she had to reckon with her uncle, who was inflexibly opposed to the marriage because an alliance with Spain was essential. Louis reluctantly accepted his duty, but wrote as many as 10 letters a day to Marie, who had been sent away. The Cardinal remained unmoved. To break up the romance, he pushed another of his nieces, Olympe, into Louis' arms, and arranged to have Marie know about it. Stung, she consented to marry a prince of the house of Colonna, and returned to Italy.

The anonymous print, directly below, exalts the deeds of the "Grande Mademoiselle" who took the city of Orléans during the Fronde. *In helmet and armor, the enterprising lady is shown sweeping away Mazarin. The caption under the picture exhorts the French to follow her example so that France can be freed from corruption and greed. Bottom of page: Portraits of three of Mazarin's nieces by an unknown 17th-century painter. At the right is Marie (1640-1715), who married Prince Colonna. It is thought that the other two are Olympe (1639-1708), who in 1657 married the Comte de Soissons, head of the French branch of the House of Savoie, and Hortense (1646-1699), who married the future Duc de Mazarin and later became a favorite at the English court.*

ALONE AT LAST

Below: Detail of a tapestry woven from a painting by Yvert the Elder, showing the coronation of Louis XIV. This took place in Reims Cathedral on June 7, 1654, with the archbishop of Soissons officiating. The French "Sacre du Roi" is a ceremony roughly equivalent to a regular royal coronation, but with certain minor differences.

It represents the mystical marriage of his "most Christian" majesty with Christian France and with the Church. The King, with his vow, undertakes to exterminate heretics and binds himself closely to the Church, which watches over orthodoxy and the spiritual life of the country.

Louis XIV was keenly aware of how much he owed Mazarin; nonetheless, the Cardinal's death, when the King was 23, brought a blessed relief. He could at last get on with the job alone. The morning after his minister's death he had already resolved never again to have a prime minister, nor to admit a churchman, a noble or a soldier to his council—no churchman, because he would have an eye on the Pope; no soldier, because his solution to a diplomatic problem would invariably be a declaration of war; no noble, because the king would merely appear to be a super-noble, whereas with the "bourgeois" there could be no confusion of rank. Henceforth his ministers' function would be to advise, not to initiate. The personal reign had begun. The "Grand Monarque" did not emerge overnight, but certainly a solid basis for this future role was set immediately. When asked by high officials to whom they should submit matters of importance, he replied, "To me." Louis found himself the ruler of the most powerful nation in Europe: 18,000,000 Frenchmen against Italy's 6,000,000, England's 5,500,000, Holland's 2,000,000, Russia's 14,000,000. The old Hapsburg Empire—a conglomeration of separate states—had a population of 21,000,000, but its political power had been fragmented, by the Peace of Westphalia and the Treaty of the Pyrenees, into countless small states: principalities, dukedoms, free cities, all wrangling with one another. France easily towered over her European neighbors, just as Louis, in terms of power and popularity, towered over his fellow rulers. He had stated categorically that "a King who cannot govern is unfit to reign." His council had readily agreed, fully expecting him to tire of the game within a week. He never did. He had many physical assets for the role he now assumed. He was young, and possessed boundless energy. He looked and acted like a king. Contemporary memoirs abound in the descriptions of his majesty. He was handsome, courtly, charming, a good dancer, a fair musician, a superb horseman, a brilliant conversationalist. His subjects viewed his assumption of full power with undisguised joy. They were tired of the miseries of civil war, of a foreign prime minister, of churchmen. They were ready to accept unquestioningly the absolute authority of their young king. As Voltaire said a century later, "If Louis XIV had not existed, it would have been necessary to invent him."

ANOTHER SPANISH MARRIAGE

Before leaving this vale of tears—and there were fewer tears for him than for most—Mazarin had made provisions for completing his task. One of these was to give his royal pupil a wife. Having broken up the idyll between his niece, Marie, and the young King, the astute Mazarin had set the stage for what came to be known as the "Comedy of Lyons." It was called thus because this city was the setting for the little comedy. The plot was simple: Louis would pretend that he was wooing his cousin, Marguerite de Savoie. This, it was hoped, would force the Spanish King to offer his daughter as a bride for Louis XIV. The Infanta Maria Teresa would bring a large dowry and, more important, peace. The comedy was a success; Spain fell in with French plans and hastened to send an envoy to the frontier of the Pyrenees to meet the French envoy. For five months, on a small island in the Bidassoa River, Mazarin, representing France, and Don Luis de Haro, representing Spain, doggedly hammered out clause after clause of the Peace of the Pyrenees. France came off rather better than did Spain. She won important territorial concessions and the promise of a large dowry for the Infanta. Spain secured the condition that, upon her marriage, the future Queen of France would waive her rights over Spain and Spanish possessions. But the prize morsel, for France, was the penalty clause Mazarin had inserted. Should the Spanish King fail to pay any portion of the dowry, the Infanta would retain her rights of succession. Philip IV had also stipulated that Condé should be pardoned, and his possessions and honors restored to him. The agreement was signed in November, 1659, and celebrated with great pomp the following June by the wedding, at Saint-Jean-de-Luz, of the King of France, Louis XIV and the Infanta of Spain, henceforth known as Marie-Thérèse. It was a marriage of cousins, another mixing of dynastic blood. There was much good-will, at least on the French side. The Queen Mother, who, despite everything, had remained much attached to her native country, was overjoyed. The King's subjects, apparently, were equally pleased, and Louis was happy with his little bride. Nor was his pleasure in any way marred by the failure of his father-in-law to pay even a fraction of the dowry that had been so readily promised. On the contrary. Louis joyfully seized on this pretext, some years later, to establish the rights of his Queen to the Spanish succession.

Above: Tapestry, designed by Testelin, of the wedding of King Louis and Philip IV's eldest daughter. The Archbishop of Bayonne performed the ceremony on June 9, 1660. Left: Tapestry, woven from a painting by Mathieu the Elder, of the betrothal of Louis XIV with the Infanta of Spain. The meeting of the two kings and their respective courts took place two days before the wedding in a room specially built for the occasion on the Island of Pheasants, neutral ground in the Bidassoa River. The marriage contract and the wedding served to ratify the Peace of the Pyrenees, which had been signed the previous winter. And so, after a 12-year delay, peace was finally established between Spain and France. The Peace of Westphalia had failed to achieve this happy state because of Spain's interference in the French Civil Wars. Mazarin's pride and pleasure in the event were well justified, for the alliance between the two countries was the reward of years of patient work. The French King, followed by his mother, the Cardinal and other members of the court, bows to Philip IV. Behind Philip stands the Infanta, Maria Teresa. This was not the most cordial of meetings. The Spaniards snubbed the French and their nouveau-riche elegance. Even the exchange of presents before the wedding had been a source of friction. Louis XIV had been generous, as had the Queen. She had sent her brother a diamond necklace. In exchange she was given a few pairs of Spanish gloves. This niggardliness, coming on top of frequent Spanish interference in French affairs, wounded Louis' pride, and made him feel that France, in his person, had been slighted.

THE SQUIRREL AND THE SERPENT

Below, left: Portrait of Nicolas Fouquet (1615-1680). He was tried before a special court of 22 judges, who, on December 20, 1664, exiled him and confiscated his property. The King commuted the verdict to life imprisonment, but allowed him the consoling company of a member of his family. Below: View of the gardens of the Château of Vaux-le-Vicomte, one of Fouquet's estates.

Nicolas Fouquet, the all-powerful superintendent of French finance, had on his coat of arms a nimble squirrel on a field of silver and the Latin motto: *Quo non ascendam?* ("To what heights may I not climb?"). In plain words, he placed no limits to his personal ambition. As soon as Mazarin had entrusted him with the finances of the country, Fouquet had started to amass a large fortune by falsifying accounts and pocketing revenues due the royal treasury. Like so many unscrupulous financiers, Fouquet was a delightful man. He was learned, generous, a discerning collector, and a tireless builder. His château of Vaux-le-Vicomte, designed by the leading French architect, Le Vau, decorated by the painter Le Brun, and landscaped by Le Nôtre, is still a masterpiece of the period. Only Versailles surpasses it. It took 18,000 laborers five years to complete it at a cost of 18 million francs. This was the immediate cause of Fouquet's downfall. In a moment of misguided optimism (although he knew Louis suspected him of fraud), he invited the king and the court to a celebration at Vaux. The magnificence of the buildings, furnishings, and grounds far surpassed anything Louis had ever seen. Perhaps the greatest irritant was the solid gold service that was used for the occasion. Louis had been obliged to have his own melted down to defray the last remaining expenses of the Thirty Years' War. Nineteen days later, Louis XIV ordered his Captain of the Guard, Charles de Baatz,

Left: Portrait of Jean-Baptiste Colbert (1619-1683). Louis XIV's ablest minister laid the foundations of French industry. His goal was to make France the richest country in Europe. He initiated public works and encouraged colonization. His eventual failure to keep France on an even financial keel was due to his inability to check the King's extravagance. Below: The Louvre, shown in a print by Jacques Callot. This part-time royal residence was enlarged and improved by Colbert.

Sieur d'Artagnan (of *The Three Musketeers*' fame), to arrest Fouquet. The embezzling minister was duly convicted and imprisoned in the fortress of Pignerol, where he remained until his death in 1680. Jean-Baptiste Colbert was in large part responsible for Fouquet's downfall, for he had echoed and re-echoed Mazarin's warning about the Finance Minister's fraudulent activities. Unlike Mazarin, whose methods were the same as Fouquet's, Colbert was incurably honest. His coat of arms bore a serpent. He was born in Reims in 1619, the son of a draper. Colbert had early learned in his father's shop the importance of good accounting—*i.e.*, that profits exist only if earnings exceed expenditures. When he was 20 he went to Paris, where he found employment first in the Ministry of War, then later with Mazarin, who trusted him implicitly. Mazarin is reputed to have said to the King on his deathbed, "Sire, I owe you everything, but I believe I can repay some of my debt by giving you Colbert." Colbert was the first man to make "the budget a balance sheet, not a statistical anthology." He worked to make France economically self-sufficient. His greatness lies in his ability to see all of France's problems as part of a whole picture. He realized there was no point in achieving a sound internal fiscal administration and promoting a free exchange of goods if there were no adequate means of communication. Hence the new roads and the admirable system of French inland waterways that he began.

LE.ROY.LOVIS.XIIII.VISITANT.LES
MANVFACTVRES.DES.GOBELINS.OV.LE
SIEVR.COLBERT.SVRINTENDANT.DE.SES
BASTIMENS.LE.CONDVIT.DANS.TOVS.LES

LUXURY, PRODUCT OF FRANCE

Colbert's name remains more closely linked with the industrial development of his country than with its fiscal improvement—an improvement that became more ephemeral with each war. Commercial agreements were concluded with Sweden and with Denmark. New companies were established to trade with the East and West Indies. In order to keep up all these activities, quality goods, mostly luxuries, had to be produced for export. To achieve this, there sprang up large corporations that were completely state controlled. It was the government that set wages, prices, and found markets for the goods. Any failure to abide by the regulations was severely punished. A work day was 12 hours long with a half-hour break for meals. The daily wages were 12 "soldes"—worth about 13 pounds of bread. The number of holidays was reduced to 38, which, added to the 52 Sundays of the year, made 90 days of annual rest. The best quality work was doubtless achieved by the Gobelin tapestry makers. But Colbert did not neglect other manufactures. He granted certain monopolies to French industry and set up protective tariffs for their benefit. He also encouraged and promoted scientific and technical teaching. He attracted to France, with generous prizes, the best European artisans available: glass-makers from Murano were settled in Saint-Gobain, Dutch weavers in Abbeville, Lombard silk weavers in Lyons. Within a few years, the ships of the French merchant marine, which had been built up by Colbert, were in a position to visit ports throughout the entire world to sell, for gold, Murano glass, Genoa lace, Delft pottery, English wool and other products. The France of Louis XIV and Colbert was in the process of achieving not only political and military supremacy but also commercial supremacy—an accomplishment not at all to the liking of England or Holland.

Left: One of a series of tapestries, produced by the Gobelin factory, commemorating the achievements of Louix XIV. This one shows the King, accompanied by Colbert, on a visit to the factory. The series was designed by Charles Le Brun (1619-1690), who was the director and chief designer. Among those who worked with him were his nephew Van der Meulen, Yvert the Elder, and Mathieu the Elder, Testelin and Seve the Younger.

ALL THE KING'S MEN

Louis XIV wrote in his *Reflections:* "I must spread my confidence and entrust the execution of my orders to various people. Each one must be employed according to his talents without ever having sole responsibility. This is the first and greatest task of a prince." He surrounded himself with associates who were as hard-working as he was. In order to keep state secrets from becoming known, in 54 years of personal reign, he managed to keep by him the same group of men, usually replacing them with their sons when the need arose. The most important trio was Colbert, Lionne, Le Tellier. Saint-Simon, the famous chronicler of court gossip during Louis XIV's reign, labeled them "vile bourgeois upstarts." Colbert's power was held in check by his two colleagues, the minister of war and the minister of foreign affairs. When Le Tellier died, his son, Louvois, replaced him. Louvois, who remodeled the French army, is not only one of the most important figures in French military history but also in that of Western Europe. "He was the greatest brute that ever lived," and was responsible for most of the French military atrocities of Louis' reign, but he created an army whose tactical and administrative methods remained almost unchanged until modern times. He set up an efficient provisioning system, created grades to which officers could be promoted without purchasing their commissions, established a fixed rate of pay, introduced the bayonet (invented by Vauban) and the flintlock rifle, and arranged the close coordination of the artillery and the corps of engineers with the infantry. During his ministry, the French army became the most powerful military force in Europe. Sébastien Le Prestre, Marquis de Vauban, also contributed to French military power. During his lengthy career as commissary-general for fortifications—from 1655 to 1707—he restored 300 strongholds, set up 33 new ones, directed 53 sieges and introduced innovations all along the line. But troops and forces would not have been enough without good generals. Turenne was the most outstanding one. He won a number of brilliant victories at the end of the Thirty Years' War and defeated even the Great Condé at the battle of the Dunes in Flanders in 1658. He was Marshal during the War of Devolution and Commander of the Army of Holland in 1674. He was killed at Sassbach in 1675 at the age of 64.

Below: Painting by an unknown artist of the French 17th-century school entitled: "Louis XIV in front of the Grotto of Thetis." It was on this grotto, done in the Italian style, that the solar emblem was used for the first time. Later, when the court had been forced into a semblance of piousness, a chapel was built on the site of the grotto. The painting dates from the first period at Versailles, when festivities were held mostly out-of-doors. The park was soon filled with allegorical statues upon which worked a number of sculptors mobilized by Le Brun. La Quintinie, in charge of the royal grounds, planted 31 trellised gardens. To the south of the recently opened canal was a zoo of exotic animals; to the north, a Chinese pavilion. In 1674, Louis XIV, proud of the finished work, compiled a guide for the use of guests at Versailles.

BUILDING FEVER

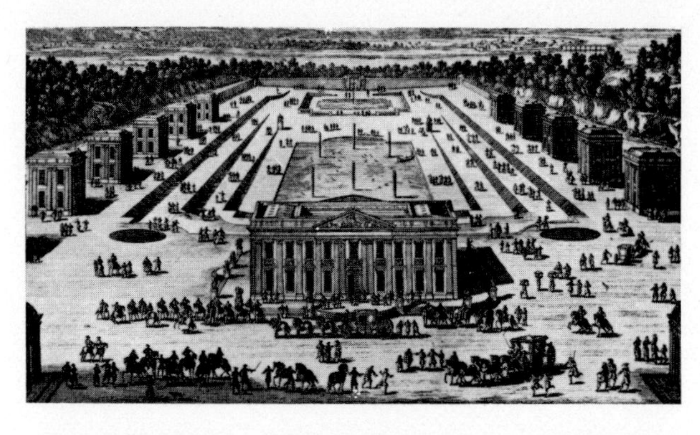

Even though Colbert had caused the Louvre to be enlarged, Louis XIV disliked his Parisian residence, reminder of too many unpleasant events. With Saint-Germain having become too small for his needs, the king looked for a building site on which to erect a remote and stately residence. Twenty years were to pass before the choice fell on Versailles, where his father had had a modest hunting lodge. The Château de Vaux was taken as a first model, and the platoon of artists who had worked on it for Fouquet moved over to the service of the King: Le Nôtre for gardens, Le Vau for architecture, Le Brun for painting and decorating. Work was begun in 1661. Le Vau remained in charge until his death in 1670. The architect Hardouin-Mansart succeeded him in 1677, but it was not until May, 1682, that the court was able to settle into the new palace. Mansart was still remodeling the apartments as late as 1701. After he died in 1708, his brother-in-law, Robert de Cotte, finished the chapel. Versailles was a lifelong undertaking for Louis XIV. Once he had contracted stone fever he was never cured of it. First came the gardens; then year after year a whole royal city grew up. The original plan had been to change the course of the Eure River in order to supply the ponds, streams and fountains, but the war of 1688 and lack of funds intervened. At Colbert's death, in 1683, Louvois became the superintendent of works and conducted a great building operation on all fronts simultaneously. An army of 36,000 bricklayers and 6,000 horses was employed. In one of her letters Madame de Sévigné, the wittiest letter writer of the court, wrote of the "prodigious mortality rate of the workmen." Every night, she said, whole cartloads of corpses were removed, as from a hospital. It is not known exactly how much Versailles cost, but it is certain that it swallowed up millions. The price of a king's grandeur was undoubtedly high. It also gave rise to inconveniences of a practical nature. Having been built for life in the open, Versailles was deficient in hygienic facilities. Odd corners, behind stairs and curtains, were used for urgent needs by the thousands of inhabitants. In short, the Palace of Versailles did not always smell of roses.

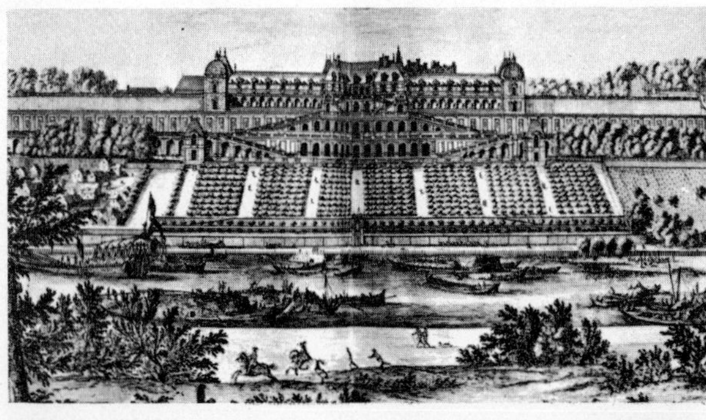

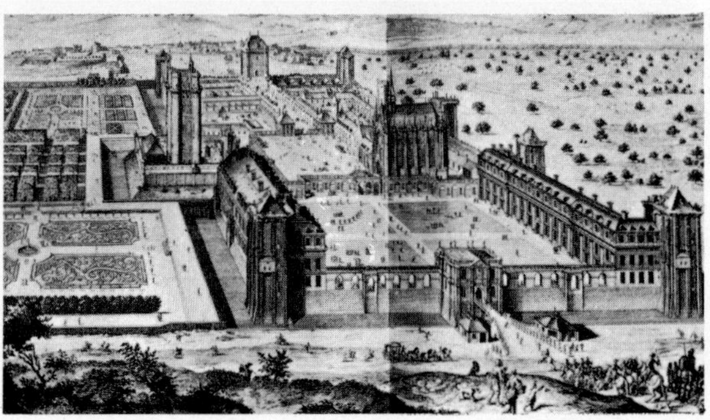

Upper left: Marly, six miles from Versailles, was one of Louis' favorite residences. He had Mansart build a central pavilion for himself adorned with the solar emblem. There were twelve lesser pavilions, with the signs of the zodiac, for the court and guests. Marly was destroyed during the French Revolution. Lower left: Four prints from a series, by Israel Silvestre (1612-1691), of the royal residences. They are, upper left: Saint-Germain-en-Laye; upper right: the palace of Fontainebleau seen from the "White Horse" courtyard; lower left: Fontainebleau again, seen from the lake; lower right: Vincennes Palace. Below: Versailles as it looked in 1722, seven years after the death of the Sun King. The painting is by Pierre Denis Martin (1673-1742), a pupil of Van der Meulen. He painted hunting and battle scenes as well as royal residences. A relative of his, Martin "of the battles," succeeded Van der Meulen as official painter of the King's victories.

In the tapestry at the right, by Dulin, Louvois is trying to show the King plans for the Hôtel des Invalides. The construction of this home for soldiers, wounded and disabled in wars fought in the service of the King, was authorized by Louis XIV in April, 1670. The architect for the project was Libéral Bruant. The work was begun in 1671. Jules Hardouin-Mansart (1648-1708) soon replaced him. He enlarged the original, somewhat primitive, plan and added the church with its high cupola. It is here, as has been noted elsewhere, that Napoleon's ashes rest. The Invalides also contains the army museum. Hardouin-Mansart started to work for Louis in 1674. His first job was to alter and improve Saint-Germain. Then, after he had been appointed the King's architect-in-chief, he took on the job of completing Versailles. Among his other works are L'Orangerie and the Grand Trianon in Versailles. He also designed the Place Vendôme in Paris, a superb example of city planning.

VERSAILLES, THE LIVING HEART OF FRANCE

Today Versailles is beautiful and empty, impressive and sad. Let us imagine 300 years ago, when it was alive and teeming with 5,000 people of rank, and as many dependents. They played their part in the continuous performance of daily court ritual, which was their only role in the government. French aristocracy still exuded a faint aroma of the stables. Uprooted from their estates, the nobles were making haphazard efforts to become civilized. Fashion in dressing was elaborate, but hygiene was unbelievably crude. Sometimes the King shaved, sometimes he did not; he washed his hands and face only occasionally. However, at Versailles, it was essential to be seen. The words "He is never seen," uttered by the King, were a condemnation. Readmitted to the court after a long period of disgrace, the Marquis de Vardes said: "Sire, away from you one is not only unhappy; one is ridiculous." The Duc de Richelieu exclaimed: "I should rather die than not see the King for two or three months!" Louis liked his courtiers to gamble. Gambling debts were another means of keeping the nobles under his thumb. Idle noblemen became useful ornaments; tamed, they vied with each other for positions and pensions. Versailles was a strange mixture of splendor and disorganization. One could come and go undisturbed. Thieves abounded, despite the watchfulness of a secret police that never succeeded in barring the way to loiterers, servants, prostitutes and hawkers. Good manners mingled with crudeness, religion with black magic. Forks were beginning to be used, yet everyone spat everywhere. People greeted each other with great courtesy, but sang vulgar songs. These were the contrasts of Versailles, the living heart of France.

Bottom of page, far left: Louis XIV at morning prayers. This took place before the court, as shown in this miniature from a Book of Hours belonging to the King. Next, the King's "lever," at which the greatest nobles of France helped dress him.
Right: The Grande Gallerie at Versailles as it appeared in the early 18th century. During the last years of Louis XIV's reign the fashion in dress became somewhat less ornate than it had been in the latter half of the 17th century. The men's clothes in particular became simpler and more graceful.

The six fashion plates immediately below belong to a series of "figures de mode" all done by Antoine Watteau (1684-1721). He was famous not only for his drawings and engravings but also for his paintings. His favorite subjects were pastoral gaieties and refined, graceful, lordly figures.

THE KING'S ACTIVITIES: A DAY-LONG SPECTACLE

Saint-Simon wrote in his memoirs that with a calendar and a watch in hand one could tell, wherever one happened to be, what Louis XIV was doing at just that moment. There undoubtedly was, in Louis XIV's make-up, a Spanish side that led him to consider life—at least his—as a work of art to be admired by one and all. It was essential that the court be allowed to appreciate that spectacle and that each courtier regulate his timetable accordingly. Breakfast, which used to be eaten by his simpler ancestors at 7 A. M., was postponed until noon. Dinner was moved ahead to 5 P. M., and supper, to midnight. The life of the court was to revolve, like a satellite, about the Sun King. Idolatry for Louis, demonstrated by the simple joy of beholding him, was a daylong occupation. Louis XIV got up late in the morning. When he awoke, his courtiers were supposed to gather round to witness the extraordinary sight of the rising of that sun. Then Mass was said. After the religious ceremony the King breakfasted, and then retired to his council chamber. Later came dinner. Louis sat alone at his small table, but the courtiers, his mistresses and his servitors were expected to be present. This was followed by a stroll through the gardens before returning to work. Often there were hunts. And at the end of the day the King took part in the court pastimes: cards, billiards, dances, receptions, concerts, etc. A supper gathering concluded this hard day's work. Fashions in dress kept changing, becoming increasingly fancy. The men started by shaving off their beards, leaving only their moustaches, and around 1670, when the King noticed that he was doomed to baldness, *perruques* (elaborately curled wigs) were introduced. A contemporary wrote, delicately if ambiguously: "It was possible to tell the women from the men only when it was time to go to bed." Adultery was condoned. Marriage for the most part was a business enterprise, a merger of names, real estate and fortunes. The spouse who found such an arid life unbearable was permitted a few "compensatory escapades." And the example was set from above. Prostitution was officially banned, but courtesans abounded. Ninon de Lenclos, one of the most charming of these, held open house. Her salon became the meeting place of writers, wits and philosophers. She entertained all the well-known figures of her day, among them Condé, Corneille, La Rochefoucauld and Saint-Simon, who described her as a "shining example of the triumph of vice . . . directed with intelligence and redeemed by a little virtue."

Opposite page: Portrait of Louis XIV by Henri Testelin. The artist had painted an earlier one of the King as a child. Here Louis is shown, scepter in hand, in all his regal splendor. This painting, like so many others, shows signs of the increasingly evident Divine Cult that was growing up around the Sun King. Left, top and bottom: Two typical moments in court life. The print immediately to the left shows the music room at Versailles. Louis XIV was an accomplished harpsichordist and guitarist, and always enjoyed concerts. In the print at the bottom of the page, the King is shown holding a public hearing. He wrote: "I have given my subjects the opportunity of coming to me in person at any hour."

Above: Tapestry by Pierre Seve the Younger (1623-1695), showing Louis XIV receiving the Spanish Ambassador, Count of Fuentes. During this interview, which took place on March 24, 1662, the Spanish envoy announced to the French King that henceforth French ambassadors at foreign courts would take precedence over Spanish ones. This was one of the details that fitted into Louis' plan to achieve international prestige. In line with this were the results of a skirmish that took place in Genoa in 1684 between French and Spanish envoys. Although the Doge was not permitted to leave the territory of the Republic, Francesco Maria Imperiali Lercaro was obliged to go to Venice with a suite of four senators to make public reparation and ask the Sun King's pardon for the incident.

Tournaments had long since given way to carrousels (a species of cavalry maneuvers and games). During the reign of Louis XIV these horseback exhibitions became an excuse for elaborate costumes and complicated steps.
Below: Prints, done by Jacques Bailly for the King, which show some of the horsemen who took part in the lavish display of 1662. This took place in what was, and still is, appropriately named the Place du Carrousel.

Prints showing two moments in court life at Versailles. Left: The King playing billiards with members of his family. Right: The King dancing a minuet at one of the many parties given at court.

LOUIS XIV STYLE

Louis left the imprint of his style on furniture as well as on other things. The style Louis XIV is divided into three periods: the early runs from 1643 to 1655; the middle from 1656 to 1694; the late from 1695 to 1715. The best known of these is the middle period, when Le Brun was director of the Royal Manufacture of furniture. The chief characteristics were ornateness and massiveness. Elaborate carving and gilded wood predominated, with marquetry of tortoise shell, and brass and gilt bronze mounting. Some attempt was made to follow classical lines.

On these two pages are reproduced some examples of furniture in Louis XIV style. Opposite page: a solid desk with the characteristic eight legs. Upper left and right: Dresser and wardrobe designed by André-Charles Boulle (1642–1732). The furniture made by this famous cabinetmaker is noted for the richness of its carving. The wardrobe shown below was designed for a man's clothing. Below left: Walls hung with elaborately embroidered clothing probably woven with gold and silver threads. Fashion often changed, but not in the degree of its gaudiness and magnificence.

DREARY EXISTENCE OF THE COMMON PEOPLE

Charles Le Brun, the leading painter of the reign of Louis XIV, left his imprint on all the forms of art produced in France during his lifetime. As director of the Gobelins he controlled the industrial arts. Through the Academy of Painting and Sculpture (of which he was co-founder) he controlled the fine arts. His own style was emphatic and pompous and in complete harmony with Louis' taste. It was typical of him to criticize Caravaggio (a 16th-century Italian naturalist painter) for having lowered the tone of a "Nativity" by painting in it two animals so lacking in nobility as the ass and the ox. Louis XIV had such a deep-rooted aversion to Dutch and Flemish masters, whose subjects he considered too lowly for his royal gaze, that he ordered his dwellings stripped of all those "little monstrosities." There remains, consequently, only a meager pictorial record of the life and condition of the common people during his reign. The pictures in question were done during the first half of the 17th century. The paintings reproduced on these two pages are by Louis Le Nain (1593–1645), the best known of three brothers, all painters. Left: peasants in their family dwelling. Right: the forge of a village blacksmith. There are other documents by engravers and etchers; for example, those of Jacques Callot whose work influenced later artists. The "Fair at Gondreville," to the left, is one of his best-known works.

POISON FOR THE ROYAL FAMILY?

Below, left: Christening of "Monseigneur le Dauphin," painting by Claude Christophe (1667–1746). The State ceremony took place on March 24, 1668. Cardinal Barbarin, great Almoner of France, performed the ceremony. Cardinal Vendôme stood as proxy for the Pope, who was godfather. The little Princesse de Conti was a proxy-godmother for Henrietta-Anne of England, daughter of Charles I of England. She was also Louis XIV's sister-in-law through her marriage to his brother, Philippe d'Orléans. Below: Print by Nicolas Arnoult showing the family of the Dauphin.

The King had had great hopes for his son, the Dauphin, born in 1661. Much thought had been devoted to the boy's education: Louis had written his *Memoires* for the latter's guidance, and had chosen Bossuet to be his tutor. This prelate, the greatest religious orator of his era, gave up most of his other activities in order to give his undivided attention to young Louis of France. The 64 volumes edited for his royal pupil cost 400,000 livres. The effort was all in vain. The Dauphin was dull-witted, heavy, and generally uninspiring. In 1680 he married Marie-Anne of Bavaria. He died in 1711, leaving three sons. Louis XIV then turned his hopes on the second "Dauphin," the Duc de Bourgogne, born in 1682. Fénelon, another literary churchman, was put in charge of the education of the young duke and of his two brothers, the dukes of Berry and of Anjou. (The latter was to become Philip V of Spain.) Their tutor wrote a variety of books for them, the best known one being the *Adventures of Telemachus*, which had 20 editions in 1699, the year it was first published. But bad luck plagued Louis XIV in his heirs; death mowed down members of the royal family one after the other. The five brothers and sisters of the Grand Dauphin had died in infancy. Particularly tragic was the year 1712, when both the Duke and Duchess of Burgundy died. Some of their children died before them, some after them. The sole survivor was a two-year-old infant, the future Louis XV. Such a high mortality rate began to look suspect to contemporaries. The word "poison" was whispered, and the accused were the Hapsburgs and the Duke of Orléans. But the suspicions seem to be unfounded. There had been an outbreak of measles, which, in those days of non-existent sanitary precautions, usually proved fatal to its victims.

A FAMILY OF DIVINITIES

This painting is by Jean Nocret (1615–1672), who worked with Mignard after having been apprenticed to Poussin. The large canvas is catalogued "Ten Members of the family of Louis XIV." But its original title, "An Assembly of Gods and Goddesses" (guess which are which), is perhaps more appropriate. The theme is clear: If the King really is a god on earth, all his relations must be divinities. In this terrestrial Olympus we see Louis XIV crowned with laurel and with the attributes of Apollo. The other man of the family "Monsieur," his brother, appears as Pluto. Surrounding Apollo-King are the ladies of the divine family: Anne of Austria as Cybele (the mother of the gods); Marie-Thérèse, the King's wife as Juno; Henrietta, daughter of the King of England, as Flora; her mother as Amphytrite, the queen of the sea; Mlle de Montpensier, the King's cousin, as Diana, and another cousin, Mlle d'Orléans, as one of the three graces. No one knows who the numerous infants are supposed to be. There were so many Bourbon offspring, legitimate and illegitimate, that it is difficult not to lose count. However, it is thought that the portrait of the two babies, at the feet of the King, is of two of his legitimate children who died in infancy.

THE KING'S MISTRESSES

Louis XIV's first love, as we have already seen, was Marie Mancini, one of Mazarin's nieces. Like so many first loves, it was a never-to-be-forgotten one. He had already had a few light amorous adventures with ladies and damsels of the Court. His mother seemed not to be opposed to these brief attachments. She was, however, very much annoyed by his pursuit of Marie Mancini. With the help of Mazarin, she put an end to the affair and succeeded in making Louis marry the Spanish Infanta, Maria Teresa, a pretty, virtuous, stupid young woman who, unfortunately for her peace of mind, fell in love with her husband on their wedding night and remained deeply in love with him until the end of her life.

At the time of their marriage the King and his new Queen were 22. Madame de Montespan, who had a poisonous tongue among other unlovable traits, said that the young Queen, whose retinue included a blackamoor dwarf, had given birth to a very dark-skinned baby who had died immediately. This was purely malicious gossip. However, there is no doubt about Louis' frequent infidelities. They seemed to be almost a social obligation. His second infatuation was with his sister-in-law, Henrietta of England, daughter of Charles I and wife of his effeminate brother Philippe. They had been married in 1661. "Madame," as she was known, was a charming, vivacious, witty young woman. In order to cover up their innocent meetings, Henrietta decided that Louis should pay ostentatious court to one of her own ladies in waiting, Louise de La Vallière, a slender, shy, slightly lame, romantic 17-year-old girl. But La Vallière fell deeply, genuinely in love with the King. Touched by her fragile blonde beauty, Louis returned her passion and made her his mistress. This fact was tacitly announced by a series of splendid fêtes given at Versailles in July 1661. For Louise it was to be a tender, disinterested love, whose only lasting reward perhaps has been the kindly verdict of history. Louise de La Vallière never capitalized on her position; she neither asked nor gave favors, she refused expensive presents, avoided cliques and intrigues. Faithful and modest in bearing, she never stopped loving Louis, even after she had been ruthlessly supplanted. She had four children by him, the first two of whom died soon after birth. Louise de La Vallière and the King lived happily and contentedly until 1667, when the scheming and unscrupulous Marquise de Montespan brought their idyll to an end.

Opposite page: Portrait of Marie-Thérèse of Austria, by an unknown painter of the 17th century. She was born in Madrid in 1638. When she died, Louis XIV said that it was the only thing she had ever done to displease him. Proud and pious, she contributed, at least in her own circle, to raising the moral tone of the court.

Above: A 19th-century print, done from a drawing by Horace Vernet, of Louis XIV's meeting with Louise de La Vallière at the Carmelite Convent in Chaillot. Right: Portrait of Louise de La Vallière painted at the height of her affair with the King. Their two surviving children were legitimized: the Comte de Vermandois and the very beautiful Mademoiselle de Blois.

Below: Contemporary etching of the witch and poisoner Voisin, who was burned at the stake in 1680. Catherine Monvoisin, better known as "la Voisin," had many famous clients, among them Madame de Montespan (Louis' mistress), Olympe Mancini (one of Mazarin's nieces), and the Comtesse de Gramont. Right: Portrait of Françoise Athénaïs de Rochechouart,

Marquise de Montespan, with four of the seven or eight children she bore the King. Born in 1641, she died in 1707 in the château to which she had retired after having left Versailles. Her fall from grace, which finally occurred in 1679, was spurred by Bossuet's remonstrances to the King and especially by the scandal that arose as the result of a police inquiry into black magic and poisoning.

Portrait of Françoise d'Aubigné, Marquise de Maintenon, by Mignard. Born in 1635, she was secretly married to Louis XIV, probably in 1684. The King had nicknamed her "Lady Reason." He often followed her advice. She died in 1719 at Saint-Cyr, to which she had retired after the death of Louis XIV.

According to Voltaire, Françoise Athénaïs de Rochechouart was one of the three most beautiful women in France. She had arrived in Paris in 1661, when she was 20, to become one of the Queen's maids of honor. Two years before, she had married the Marquis de Montespan. Later, during a stay at Compiègne, she went, by mistake, into the King's room, where she fell asleep. Always the soul of courtesy, Louis, finding her there, kept her in his bed. In 1667 Madame de Montespan became the King's official mistress, a post she held for 12 years, even though Louis strayed occasionally. La Vallière had struggled for a while to keep the King's love, but finally retired to a convent. There she lived until 1710 under the name of Soeur Louise de la Miséricorde—36 years of convent life to expiate seven years of pleasure. Left mistress of the field, Madame de Montespan showed her true colors. Intelligent, stimulating and witty, she was a stimulus for the King, but she also was wildly extravagant, grasping, selfish and jealous. From the sorceress Voisin she obtained toxic love potions, which she gave the King. But she went too far. Her connection with the poison scandal, her wit—which never spared Louis—and her total lack of maternal feeling were finally the cause of her undoing. She bore the King eight children. For the survivors of his offspring she needed a governess. Her choice fell on the converted granddaughter of a Huguenot, Françoise d'Aubigné. She was born in the prison of Niort, had emigrated to Martinique and had returned to France to work in a convent. She came to the attention of the crippled, aging author, Paul Scarron. Moved to pity by the plight of the graceful, intelligent adolescent, Scarron married her, but only to rescue her from what appeared to him a living death. Their relationship was a pleasant, affectionate one. In return for his unfailing kindness, she ran his house and looked after the elderly man. At his death he left her little money, but even so she was infinitely better off than she had been before her marriage. Later, she performed her task so well with the royal children that she came to the King's attention. (One of Louis' most endearing traits was his fondness for children.) Touched by the genuine affection she showed for her young charges, and impressed by her intelligence, integrity and good sense, the King gave her a present of money. With this she bought the land and title of the Marquisate of Maintenon. Ten years later she became Louis' morganatic wife.

Portrait of Henrietta of England by Mathieu. The 16-year-old bride of the King's brother, she was the unwitting cause of the affair between Louis XIV and La Vallière. She died at 26 on June 30, 1670, after having persuaded her brother, King Charles II of England, to ally himself with France against Holland.

THE PERIOD OF GREAT TRIUMPHS

The tapestry below, one of the series "The Story of the King," was begun by Mathieu and finished by Seve the Younger. It shows Louis XIV, holding the baton of commander, about to make his entry into Dunkirk on December 2, 1662. Dunkirk was one of Louis' first territorial acquisitions, one of the few that were peacefully obtained. The city had been ceded to England at the time of Cromwell. The King of France reacquired it from Charles II for the sum of four million livres. His first care was to have the city fortified by Vauban. The forts were later to be destroyed under the terms of the Peace of Utrecht.

The farsighted policies of Richelieu and of Mazarin had made France the greatest and most respected power in Europe. Louis XIV worked faithfully at his job as King. By making the most of his own and his counselors' talents, Louis strengthened domestic economy, developed foreign trade and increased France's international prestige. Nonetheless, he was not yet satisfied. War was the natural vocation of a King who wanted to be great. The love of glory was Louis XIV's ruling passion. Hence the key to France's foreign policy must be sought primarily in the King's psychological make-up. It may be that posterity has credited him with more forethought than he actually had. Much has been said of France's "natural frontiers": the Rhine, the Alps, the Pyrenees. But strategic frontiers rather than natural ones were more important to him and to his entourage. There were many other motivating factors for the wars he undertook: the struggle for the Spanish succession and the *idée fixe* that the peace with Spain was only a temporary truce; the political-economic repercussions of a policy of expansion that clashed with Anglo-Dutch commercial interests; the thorough exploitation of the treaties of Westphalia and of the Pyrenees; the search for European markets for French products. For the six years between 1661 and 1667, Louis XIV showed he could wait and be diplomatic. He kept up the paid friendship with his cousin and brother-in-law, Charles II of England. He signed a defensive and commercial pact with Holland; he persuaded the Duc de Lorraine to cede his province to the Crown—a concession that the Duke immediately regretted. Louis waited, but not idly. He waited for the death of his uncle and father-in-law, Philip IV, who obliged him in 1665, and for his own mother's death, the year after. He had not wanted to cause her pain. He listened to the advice of Vauban and of Louvois. The former maintained that it would be easier to defend a country owning the strongholds that controlled means of communications: highways, major rivers, strategic ports, mountain passes. Louvois prepared an efficient and well-run army. *Nec pluribus impar* ("not unequal to many") was one of Louis XIV's mottoes. To wage war, a legal motive would have to be found. It was the function of his counselors to do so, and they did.

Le Brun had commissioned some of his staff to follow the King during his campaigns so that these artists could paint, from life, actual events. These were then elaborated in the composition of the large tapestries devoted to celebrating the glory of the King. The first one to be chosen for this assignment was Le Brun's nephew, Van der Meulen. Other artists succeeded him, among them Parrocel. On these two pages are some of the most significant examples of the fruitful production of this undertaking. Left: Detail from a tapestry recording the siege of Douai in July, 1667, during the war known as the "War of Devolution." In the foreground is one of the King's guards, whose horse was killed by a cannonball shot from the trenches surrounding the town. On the right, other scenes of episodes of the campaigns of this war are depicted. Top: The taking of Lille in August, 1667. The King is shown advancing from the left, followed by members of his court. Center: The arrival in Arras of the Queen after the conquest of this key city. Bottom: The siege of Bruges, in Flanders. (The King, wearing a hat with a red plume, is at the right.)

THE QUEEN'S TERRITORIAL RIGHTS

All of Colbert's efforts to strengthen the economy eventually came to naught. The expenses incurred by a succession of wars demanded steadily increasing taxation. But even this did not suffice. The print, below left, shows public reaction to some of the government's fiscal policies. Right: Louis XIV at the siege of Mons in 1691, from a painting by Lecomte.

The King of Spain, who died in 1665, left the Low Countries (present-day Belgium) to his son, Charles II. The latter was the child of a second marriage, hence the younger half-brother of Marie-Thérèse. Because Marie Thérèse's dowry had never been paid, Louis declared war on Spain invoking an old law of Brabant, which provided that property might "devolve" upon the children of a first marriage—in this case upon Marie-Thérèse. Louvois, Turenne and Vauban prepared the offensive while the legal boys justified the coming war in masses of documents, one of which the King himself supplied: "A Treatise on the Rights of the Queen." When it was pointed out that in the marriage contract the Spanish Infanta had renounced all claims to inheritance because of her dowry of 500,000 gold ducats, the French envoy retorted that not one penny of it had been paid. On May 24, 1667, Louis XIV ordered his troops to cross the border into the Low Countries.

The French had 55,000 men, the Spaniards 8,000. It was a pushover. The King, followed by his court, entered Charleroi, Tournai, Lille. After a few days in the provinces of Flanders, Artois and Hainault, these were annexed by France. Spain asked the help of the Emperor Leopold, but the French Embassy foiled the stroke by promising to share with him the Spanish booty. Things went less well with England and with Holland. The latter had a proverb: "The French rooster is a friend, but not when he's a neighbor." A third setback was given by Sweden, which intervened against France. Louis XIV had the sense to stop. But he was not soon to forget Holland's share in these events—those proud republican burghers who monopolized the seas, interfered with French commerce and got in the way of Colbert's economic plans. However, the game was to be played again later. Meantime Louis XIV had sent Condé to occupy the province of Franche-Comté, which belonged to Spain. This move was for purposes of barter. The French King himself drew up a treaty of peace that was signed in 1668 at Aix-la-Chapelle. France gave back Franche-Comté; Spain repossessed Besançon, but gave up 12 fortified cities in the north. Thus France held on to half of her conquests, including Lille, Charleroi, Armentières—in other words, a good slice of the Low Countries. It was apparently still possible in those days to speak of profitable wars and victories.

MONS ASSIEGEE LE 15 DE MARS 1691 LA PLACE RENDVE LE
DAVRIL LE ROI COMMANDANT L'ARMÉE EN PERSONNE

VICTORIES WERE NOT SUFFICIENT

The squadron of the French admiral, Duquesne, met the Dutch-Spanish fleet at Augusta on April 22, 1676. The great Dutch admiral Ruyter was mortally wounded during the battle. In the next encounter, on June 2 off Palermo (shown in the print on the opposite page), the success of the French in the Mediterranean was decisive. Below: Two contemporary prints that satirize the wars of Louis XIV. The first one, of Dutch origin, concerns the invasion of the Low Countries and shows the Emperor, Leopold I. The second print, from a French almanac of the year 1691, lampoons William III of Orange, King of England.

A number of historians have accused Louis XIV of having plunged his country, during the latter part of his reign, into a series of dynastic wars that harmed French domestic and national interests. This may well be, but it was true that France had become too powerful for her European neighbors. During the years between the Treaty of Aix-la-Chapelle in 1668 and the Treaty of Nijmegen in 1678, Louis XIV devoted his energies to consolidating his territorial gains and to adding others, especially in the direction of Holland, against whom he declared war in 1672. But, checked by the floods the Dutch produced by opening their dikes, he had to turn to Spanish and Imperial lands. Victory followed victory for his forces. Once again he had the sense to stop the war and to accept the peace overtures the Dutch were making. Holland got off lightly in the Peace of Nijmegen, but Louis was less accommodating with Spain. From her he exacted the province of Franche-Comté and secured for himself a fortress barrier stretching from the Meuse to Dunkirk. On the debit side was the undying hatred that Holland now bore him.

There was soon to be a new and larger anti-French movement. It started as the League of Augsburg, a coalition of German states and interests. Then with the addition of Holland, England and Savoy it became known as the War of the Grand Alliance. In America it was known as King William's War. The cause of this war was a claim, put forth by Louis on behalf of his sister-in-law, to a large part of the Palatinate. He invaded and devastated this state with a thoroughness and brutality that made his contemporaries and history forget his usual humaneness and clemency. "Madame Palatine," his brother's second wife, whose deep affection for him he had always been able to count on, refused for weeks to speak to him. The war dragged on for nine years, at a cost in men and money unjustified by the results. It came to an end chiefly because all the belligerents were exhausted. The Treaty of Ryswick, signed in 1697, was Louis' first real setback on the international stage. Under its terms he lost all the territories he had conquered after 1679 except Strasbourg. The Dutch gained important commercial concessions, the independence of Savoy was granted, and William III of Orange was recognized as King of England. It was finally brought to Louis' attention that wars can be lost even when battles are won.

PATRON OF THE ARTS

Louis XIV is shown here in his role as patron of the arts. For financial reasons, however, his active interest was limited to the first half of his reign. But, even at its highest point, he never was very openhanded in his allotment of royal pensions—none ever exceeded 100,000 livres. Numerous academies were encouraged and subsidized by him and by Colbert. The most famous of these was the French Academy, founded in 1635 with the encouragement of Richelieu. Louis' policy of increasing French prestige led him to attract to France eminent foreigners, chiefly scientists. He was on good terms with contemporary writers, especially with Racine and Boileau, whom he appointed court historians. He did much to launch Molière on his career, and encouraged Bossuet and Fénelon, whom he chose to be the tutors of his son and grandson, respectively. Louis XIV's interest was not exactly selfless. As the Prussian ambassador Spanheim observed: ". . . if the King enjoys giving, he enjoys even more receiving." But Spanheim, an eminently impartial observer, noted that Louis XIV was not without talent himself. He wrote well and was a gifted musician, as well as a connoisseur of painting and architecture.

VIRGILIUS

During the meeting the French Academy held on January 27, 1687, to celebrate the King's recovery from an operation, Charles Perrault (1628-1703) read a poem that compared Louis XIV's era with that of Augustus. This was the beginning of a famous literary controversy. Later, Perrault published a pamphlet, "Parallels between the Ancients and the Moderns" (see print reproduced at the left), which was illustrated with a picture of the Sun King surrounded by the famous men of France. Perrault's name lives on because of the fairy stories he published in 1697 for his 10-year-old son. Among these are "Little Red Riding Hood," "Cinderella," "Puss-in-Boots" and "Bluebeard." Right: Some of the men who contributed to the glory of the reign of Louis XIV. The two self-portraits at the top are Philippe de Champaigne (1602-1674), of Flemish origin, and Le Brun, the court painter. Below these, left to right, the portraits of Jean Racine (1639-1699), who, with Corneille, attained the highest level of modern classical tragedy; Charles Perrault, and Nicolas Boileau-Despréaux (1636-1711), a close friend of Racine's. Boileau was a literary critic who crossed pens with Perrault. He was noted especially for his verse satires. He faithfully imitated the poetry of the Latin poet Horace.

ALL EUROPE SPOKE FRENCH

Not since the days of Charlemagne had the greatness, power and prestige of France reached such a zenith. And Charlemagne could not properly be described as French any more than could his empire. Internal troubles, all blamed on Colbert, did not lower French prestige in foreign eyes. The French themselves fairly worshipped their King. Louis XIV was proclaimed "Great" by the Council of Paris, painted as a god by Le Brun, idealized by the common people, exalted by philosophers, envied by other kings. Europe spoke French. The language, which had been refined by the gentle art of conversation, had become rich in nuances, clarity, logic. There began that tyranny of grammar that was never to be thrown off in France. Claude Favre de Vaugelas was the first of a long series of despots in that line. Born in the Savoy, he had moved to Paris, where he wrote his observations on the spoken language. He pruned out archaic terms, and selected the best phrases in use at the time. Never did France have so many geniuses as she had during Louis XIV's century. The classicism of the period was simply another form of absolutism, this one applied to the field of the arts and of the intellect, and the State became a patron of the arts. In 1663, Colbert made up a list of persons worthy of a pension. The writer Chapelain was described as being "the greatest French poet of all times," and was assigned an annual grant of 3,000 livres (about $1,260). Who remembers Chapelain now? But there were on the pension list others whose names have survived: Corneille, Racine, Molière, Boileau. Perhaps the only great writer who did not share in the royal largesse was Blaise Pascal. He had been a libertine, a term that in his day referred to freedom of thought rather than to freedom of morality (although it could be argued that the latter was the logical consequence of the former). Pascal, a scientist and the inventor of the first computer, among other things, had been persuaded by his sister to enter the religious community of Port-Royal, a Jansenist center. The order had been founded by the Dutchman Cornelis Jansen, a bishop who wanted to reform Christian life according to the precepts of St. Augustine. The chief purpose of the movement was a return to greater personal holiness, to be achieved by divine grace and pre-destination. Although Jansenist doctrine was deeply rooted in Catholicism, the Jesuits—whom it criticized openly—accused the Jansenists of Calvinism, and finally succeeded in destroying the order.

THE LITERARY AGE OF LOUIS XIV

The etching above is one of a series that illustrate the celebrations that Louis organized for Versailles in 1674. Below: A scene from the play "Tartuffe," with Molière in the part of Orgon. The comedy was performed at court in 1664 and only once in public in 1667. It was not until 1699 that a public performance of it was sanctioned, and this only as a result of the King's intercession. Below this, the king's comedians in a scene from a farce. Right: Portrait of Molière (1622-1673) as Caesar, by Mignard.

Jean Baptiste Poquelin, better known as Molière, had inherited his father's upholstery business. But he soon abandoned it for the stage. After having directed a touring company for 15 years, he settled in Paris in 1659. It is most unlikely that the King, as has been reported, had him to dinner, but Louis was generous to him in other ways, even to the grave. Actors, whom the Church looked upon as unreclaimed sinners, were not allowed Christian burial. King Louis saw to it that his favorite playwright and actor received one.

Corneille, Racine, Molière dominated the French theater in the 17th century. Pierre Corneille was the founder of French classical tragedy. His play, *Le Cid*, which took Paris by storm, introduced a theme—the conflict between honor and love—that was to occupy French drama for nearly two centuries. He produced another four or five equally good plays, but soon wrote himself out, slipping into a monotonous and bombastic style. Jean Racine then displaced Corneille in the popular favor. Corneille's heroes, strong and rational figures, had suited French audiences during the reign of Louis XIII. The more cultivated audiences of the age of Louis XIV required drama that was elegant rather than majestic, sensitive rather than robust. Racine, educated by the Jansenists of Port-Royal, steeped in Greek civilization, wrote plays that satisfied, and perhaps even edified, the French court. His masterpieces, *Andromache*, *Britannicus*, *Phaedra*, *Athalie* and *Esther*, survive to this day.

The last member of this trio, Molière, was an actor and producer but also, and primarily, a writer of comedies. He transformed comedy, from the somewhat crude type of farce it had been, into the thoughtful, brilliant plays that became the first modern comedies of manners. He enjoyed almost continuously the favor of Louis XIV. The King's support and encouragement permitted him to produce plays that ridiculed the nobility and the clergy, who were understandably annoyed.

These were not the only authors of note. Jean de La Fontaine, with his delightful *Fables*, added considerably to the literary brilliance of the era. The fluent grace of his verse, his laconic wit and the conciseness of form of his poems have never been surpassed. The Marquise de Sévigné, with the voluminous correspondence she left, raised the art of letter-writing to unprecedented heights by her wit, elegance and acuteness of observation. And there were others: the aristocratic and disillusioned La Rochefoucauld, with his polished epigrams: "If we succeed in overcoming our passions, it is more because they are weak than because we are strong." "It takes two to make a bore." La Bruyère, the timid but astute observer of human types: the name-dropper, the aging belle, the ostentatiously busy man. It was these writers, not the generals, statesmen, grandees, who made of Louis' reign the Splendid Century.

ABSOLUTISM IN RELIGION

Absolutism, to be effective, must extend to every field. One small crack could make the whole structure crumble. It was logical, therefore, that Louis XIV should expect to control religion along with everything else. Louis was devout rather than pious, and his religion was more a fear of Hell than a love for Heaven. Although he was by definition "His Most Christian Majesty," he felt quite independent of the Pope. He had had his fill of cardinals. Mazarin and de Retz were going to last him a lifetime. He was, paradoxically, both religiously bigoted and anti-clerical. In any event, it would not have been consonant with his obsession with *la gloire* to acknowledge the Pope's superiority in any manner. However, with the passage of time and the influence, perhaps, of Madame de Maintenon, he began to take an interest in matters of faith and in the enforcement of orthodoxy. The first skirmish was against quietism, a doctrine that confused the ecstasy of the pure love of God with religion. The struggle against Jansenism was more serious. A theological dispute at first, the conflict became tinged with political overtones. More serious, however, and with far graver results, was Louis' fight against the Huguenots. At first government officials tried to force them to convert. Dragoons were billeted in Huguenot houses, where they behaved as though they were in enemy territory. There were all manner of persecutions, great and small—from the forbidding of Huguenots to practice certain professions to the banning of mixed marriages and the separation of children from their parents. Finally, in 1685, Louis revoked the Edict of Nantes, which his grandfather, Henry IV, had issued to protect the rights of the Huguenots. Retribution for this particular crime was swift. Hundreds of thousands of Huguenots emigrated. They had been the backbone of the nation. Broadly speaking, they were more intelligent, harder working and soberer than their Catholic counterparts. Their departure dealt irreparable damage to the whole structure of France; it bled the army, the navy, the legal profession, the most prosperous businesses. They took with them, and sowed in their adopted lands, a hatred for and contempt of the French that took years to wipe out. Historians have tried to put the blame for this greatest blunder of Louis XIV's on Madame de Maintenon, or on Louvois. They were, in fact, quite innocent. The culprits were the French people and the general intolerance of the times.

From left to right: Four of the leading figures involved in the events of Port-Royal: Blaise Pascal (1623-1662); the theologian Quesnel (1634-1719), whose polemics with the Archbishop of Paris aroused the papal wrath; Bossuet (1627-1704), supporter of the religious policy of the King; the Dutch Bishop Cornelis Jansen (1585-1638).

Left: The Abbey of Port-Royal as it appeared before it was destroyed. Founded in 1204 in the environs of Chevreuse, it was reformed in 1608 by Angélique Arnauld. In 1636 it became the French center of Jansenism. The Abbey, which was closed forever in 1709, was razed to the ground in 1712. Pascal had retired there in 1654. Before becoming the supporter of papal proclamations, Louis defended "Gallic freedom," or the independence of the Church of France. In 1682 a meeting of clerics approved a declaration which affirmed that the authority of the Holy See extended only to spiritual matters and that an Ecumenical Council was superior to the Pope, who was not infallible. The tapestry reproduced above illustrates an episode connected with the first phase of Louis XIV's religious policy. As the result of the killing in Rome of one of the French Ambassador's pages, the King demanded an official apology from Pope Alexander VII. Cardinal Chigi, the Pope's nephew and his envoy, is shown reading the letter of apology to King Louis XIV.

SPAIN, ETERNAL SOURCE OF TROUBLE

A long series of wars and peace treaties had not resolved the number-one problem of European politics, the succession to the Spanish throne. King Charles II of Spain was on the point of dying, without heirs. He would leave an empire that stretched from America to the Philippines and from the Low Countries to Italy. Louis XIV thought it would be a pity not to attempt to get at least a slice of it. He thought he had some rights, for he was the son of Anne, eldest daughter of Philip III; he was also the widower of Marie-Thérèse, the eldest daughter of Philip IV. In other words, he was the grandson and son-in-law of Spanish kings. However, the Emperor Leopold contested Louis' claims, for he, too, was the grandson of Philip III and the son-in-law of Philip IV, through his marriage to Marguerite, Marie-Thérèse's younger half-sister. The King and the Emperor were cousins and brothers-in-law. Why not partition Spain between them? Accordingly, they signed a secret pact on January 19, 1698. England and Holland got wind of it and objected. William of Orange proposed another partition, and Louis signed again. But the new agreement did not suit Leopold, who refused to accept it. All this signing and refusing of pacts also annoyed the dying Charles II. The latter appointed as his heir the French Dauphin's second son, Philippe d'Anjou, who had to renounce all future claim to the French throne. If Philip refused these conditions, the throne was to go to Archduke Charles, Leopold's younger son. Then, satisfied, Charles II died. Louis XIV was cornered. If he accepted the throne for his grandson, the Hapsburg Empire, England and Spain would converge upon him; if he refused he would leave the way open for Leopold. So he accepted the throne for his grandson—and war.

Below, both pages: Painting by Laguerre of the Battle of Blenheim (1704), showing the allied troops as they take up their positions before the battle. The Duke of Marlborough commanded the English forces; Prince Eugene, the Imperial ones. The encounter, in which the French were defeated, took place near the Bavarian village of Höchstädt on the Danube, which had been the scene of a battle the previous year. The prints at the bottom of the page show (left) Philip being proclaimed King of Spain and (right) an allegorical picture of the new monarch. On November 16, 1700, Louis XIV presented to the court his grandson, the Duke of Anjou, as King of Spain. The Ambassador from Madrid knelt and said, "There are no more Pyrenee Mountains between our countries." Then he escorted the young King to his new country. The Pyrenees did not disappear then or later. The Duke of Anjou, son of the "Grand Dauphin," was born at Versailles in 1683. He was not a bad king and tried to improve conditions in Spain. He died in 1746.

THE SLOW TWILIGHT OF A LONG REIGN

Above: Portrait of Prince Eugene by Jacob von Suppen. The famous imperial general, son of Olympe Mancini, was born in Paris in 1663 and died in Vienna in 1736. He had apparently been destined for the Church. Indeed it was said that, having asked Louis XIV for a command, the King retorted he didn't know what to do with "little abbots." Right: The Battle of Turin, which took place on September 7, 1706, as painted by Jacob Huchtenburg. Prince Eugene is on the white charger in the right foreground.

When Philip V became King, diplomacy was set in motion to convince King Louis he was making a mistake. His reply was to draw up an act that did not exclude Philip V from eventually becoming King of France. This meant war again. The Emperor Leopold ordered Prince Eugene of Savoy to invade France. Prince Eugene was one of the triumvirate that became the soul of the naval and land struggle; the other two were John Churchill, Duke of Marlborough, and the Dutchman Heinsuis, Louvois' old enemy. It was a world war with economic facets (whoever won would control not only European markets but also the new, and important ones, of America) and with nationalistic interests. Marlborough and Eugene of Savoy went from victory to victory; France steadily lost the territories she had acquired through preceding wars. The two generals, taking advantage of the fact that the French armies had pushed forward beyond the lines fortified by Vauban, substituted a war of movement for one of sieges, to the indignation of orthodox strategists. France was profoundly discouraged; it had lost its position—won at Rocroi—as first military power in the world. It was not to recapture this until the coming of Napoleon. The rays of the Sun King no longer warmed; they seared. Poverty, hunger and wars had in 30 years reduced the population by four million. Fénelon wrote: "Everything has collapsed, nor shall we recover from this war. In my opinion, the only possible conclusion is the purchase of an armistice at any price." In 1710, Louis sent out peace feelers. But the terms were not only that France go back to her frontiers of 1648 but also that Louis himself declare war on Spain. The aged King replied: "Since there has to be war, I prefer to wage it against my enemies rather than against my children." Meantime, profiteers were hoarding grain to make prices rise. The French got through the year 1710 by importing 5½ million pounds of grain from North Africa. But, fortunately for France, there were changes occurring in Europe. In England, with Queen Anne on the throne, the Tories had come to power. They were as eager for peace as Louis was. The unexpected death of the Emperor of Austria and the advent to the throne of the Archduke Charles VI sped up the negotiations with France. Thanks to last-minute victories won by Villars, France was able to retrieve some of her prestige at the peace conferences that followed.

THIRTEEN YEARS OF WAR FOR AN EASY PEACE

Two battles of the War of the Spanish Succession. The first, above, was fought at Oudenaarde in 1708, and ended with the defeat of the French. The second one, below, at Villaviciosa in 1711, was a French victory against Prince Eugene. The Duc de Vendôme, his cousin, is shown supervising the making of a litter, for Philip V, of the banners captured from the imperial forces. The close collaboration between Marlborough and Prince Eugene was one of the chief reasons for the allied victories during the War of the Spanish Succession. Witness to this close working relationship is the agreement (pictured to the right) signed by the two commanders in 1710 regarding the recruiting and payment of the troops.

An envoy, the Abbé Gaulthier, was secretly sent to Paris to ask if the King wanted peace. He did. Accordingly, France, England and Holland signed the Treaty of Utrecht on April 11, 1713. The long war, the last of the interminable wars waged by Louis XIV, had finally come to an end. Under the terms of this treaty, Italy and the Low Countries were given over to the Hapsburgs. Holland gave Lille back to France, but secured the right to keep garrisons in the Low Countries. Philip V was recognized King of Spain and of her colonies. Through him the Bourbons were to reign there, with one minor interruption, until 1931. France acknowledged the English succession as belonging to the House of Hanover (she had been supporting the Stuarts' claim to the English throne). England obtained Gibraltar, Minorca, Nova Scotia and Newfoundland. The Duke of Savoy was perhaps the one who made the greatest gains; Nice and Savoy were restored to him, and he acquired Sicily and a royal crown. The Bavarian Elector took back Luxembourg. France kept the province of Alsace with its key city of Strasbourg as well as Vauban's line of forts, but she was forced to raze the fortifications of Dunkirk and to fill the harbor. In effect, the Treaty reduced France's frontiers to Louis XIV's first territorial acquisitions. However, even if she was greatly weakened, France was still in a relatively strong position on the European continent, for at least she was united. Germany was still only a conglomeration of wrangling independent states, the Hapbsurgs had been held in check, and Italy was very far from achieving any sort of unity. The Emperor Charles VI continued the war, but he was seriously hampered by the defection of his allies. In 1714 he finally agreed to the treaties of Rastatt and of Baden. These complemented the general settlement achieved by the Peace of Utrecht. The only real malcontent was Eugène de Savoie, who had not seen France crushed as he had hoped. In fact, he had suffered his first major defeats at the hands of her generals. No doubt to dissociate himself as much as possible from early connections, he had taken to signing himself Eugene von Savoy. The war had been a costly one in money and men, and came to an end chiefly because of the exhaustion of the combatants. It also marked the end of an era, the era of French expansion. Henceforth England would hold the stage, and the British Empire would grow steadily, with only one setback, for over two centuries.

THE SETTING OF THE SUN

The sun had reached the end of its long course. As Louis lay dying in the last days of August, 1715, remorse and regret seemed to be uppermost in his mind. He assembled the court, for the last time, to take his farewell. "Gentlemen, I have to ask your pardon for setting you so bad an example. I thank you for the manner in which you have served me, and for the loyal attachment that you have always shown. . . . I ask you to continue to serve my great-grandson with as much zeal and fidelity as you have shown me. He is a child, and may have many unpleasantnesses in store for him. . . . Obey the commands that my nephew will give you. He is about to govern the Kingdom; I trust he will govern it well. . . . I feel that my emotions are becoming too strong for me, and I perceive that you are also moved. . . . Farewell, gentlemen, I hope you will sometimes think of me when I am gone." He dismissed them, then summoned his servants, whose pardon he also asked. As they knelt, weeping before him, he asked, "Did you think me immortal?" To Madame de Maintenon he confided the following night: "One always hears it said that it is difficult to make up one's mind to die; I don't find anything difficult about it." To his successor, his five-year-old great-grandson, he said: "You will soon be the King of a great realm. I urge you most strongly not to forget your duty to God; remember that you owe Him what you are. Try to keep the peace with your neighbors; too many people love wars; avoid my example in this respect and don't imitate my extravagance. Alleviate the suffering of your people as much as you are able, and do all the things I was unfortunate enough not to do. . . ." It was said that his mother, long ago, had said to him: "My son, be like your grandfather and not like your father." When Louis asked why, she replied: "At the death of Henry IV there was weeping; at Louis XIII's there was laughter."

The moral courage with which Louis saw the end draw near was free of the ostentation of the rest of his life. He died on September 1, at 8:15 A.M., aged 77 minus three days, after having reigned for 72 years, three months and eighteen days. "Thus passed the glory of the world, *sic transit gloria mundi*," wrote one of his servants. This verdict may sound high-flown to modern ears, but it would be difficult to find fault with the epitaph written of him two centuries later: "He walked into eternity with the same tranquil majesty with which he used to cross the Hall of Mirrors."

It was François Marie Arouet, better known as Voltaire, who vindicated the memory of the Sun King and who gave to the 17th century the name that it retains to this day: "The Century of Louis XIV." It is significant that the tireless iconoclast, the standard-bearer of revolutionary theories, the champion of individual liberty should have chosen to defend the absolute monarch in his actions. Louis was great even in the eyes of his contemporaries. Eugene of Savoy, who had ample reason for disliking him, wrote in his memoirs in 1715: "When I heard of the death of Louis XIV, I admit it had the same effect upon me as if I had heard of a splendid oak uprooted and laid flat upon the ground by a storm. He stood upright for so long! Death, before it effaces great memories, recalls them for a moment in a flash of time." Prince Eugene, however, was wrong about death's effacing this great memory. Louis still lives on. A marginal note will serve better than volumes to record one of Louis XIV's accomplishments. At the meetings that led to the signing of the Treaty of Nijmegen, French was spontaneously adopted as the common language; it was to remain, for two and a half centuries, the official language of diplomacy. Louis made France great, then and now. And with France, Europe.

1638—September 5: Born to Anne of Austria and Louis XIII at Saint-Germain-en-Laye.

1642—December 4: Death of Richelieu.

1643—May 14: Death of Louis XIII. May 18: Mazarin appointed prime minister. May 19: Defeat of the Spaniards by Condé at Rocroi.

1648—Treaty of Westphalia, which put an end to the Thirty Years' War.

1648-49—Civil War known as the *Fronde* of the *Parlement*.

1648—August 26: Pierre Broussel, President of the *Parlement*, arrested. Outbreaks of violence follow. Flight of the Queen Mother and the King to Rueil.

1649—January 8: Mazarin is outlawed by the *Parlement*. August 28: The Regent, the King and Mazarin return to Paris.

1649-53—*Fronde* of the Princes.

1650—January 18: The princes Condé, Conti and Longueville imprisoned at Vincennes by order of Mazarin for their rebellious activities. Turenne marches upon Paris, from Belgium, and is defeated by Mazarin.

1651—February 13: *Parlement* exiles Mazarin, who retires to Brühl, in Germany. Condé allies himself with Spain and negotiates with England. September 8: Louis XIV assumes full powers.

1652—July 2: Condé occupies Paris. October 21: Louis XIV returns to the capital to quiet, by his presence, the widespread unrest of the people of Paris.

1653—February 6: The King summons Mazarin back to Paris. England and France form an alliance against Spain.

1658—June 14: Spain defeated at the battle of the Dunes.

1659—November 7: Treaty of the Pyrenees between France and Spain.

1660—Louis XIV marries Marie-Thérèse of Austria, daughter of the King of Spain, Philip IV.

1661—March 9: Death of Mazarin. Fouquet, Superintendent of Finance, is stripped of his powers.

1665—Death of Philip IV of Spain, Louis' father-in-law. Louis lays claim to Belgium as his wife's portion of the inheritance. Colbert appointed Comptroller General.

1667—Sieges of Lille and Douai; conquest of Flanders by Louis XIV.

1668—January: Secret treaty of Grémonville with the Emperor. Conquest of Franche-Comté. England, Holland and Sweden form the Triple Alliance. Louis XIV proposes the peace treaty of Aix-la-Chapelle.

1672—Having made separate alliances with Sweden (Treaty of Stockholm) and with England (Treaty of Dover), Louis XIV invades Holland. The latter forms a new coalition with the Empire, Spain and Brandenburg. French forces cross the Rhine at Tholuis.

1674—While Condé is fighting in Belgium, the King occupies Franche-Comté.

1676-77—War drags on along the Rhine, in Holland and on the coasts of Sicily.

1678-79—Treaty of Nijmegen. Treaty of Alliance of Saint-Germain with Brandenburg.

1681—Annexation of Strasbourg.

1683—Louis XIV besieges Luxembourg. Spain declares war on him.

1684—August 15: Truce of Ratisbon between France and Spain.

1685—Revocation of the Edict of Nantes. Resumption of persecutions against the Protestants.

1686—Formation of the League of Augsburg, a partial coalition of defense against France.

1688—Louis XIV orders his troops to occupy the Palatinate.

1689-97—War of the League of Augsburg. Louis XIV attempts in vain to put James II back on the English throne by force of arms. He takes up again the offensive on the Rhine, in Italy and in Holland. After a series of victories he concludes hostilities with the Treaty of Ryswick.

1700—Upon the death of Charles II of Spain the Duc d'Anjou, Louis XIV's grandson, becomes King of Spain as Philip V.

1701—September: Before dying, William III of England forms the Great Alliance with Holland, the Empire and a little later Savoy and Portugal.

1701-13—War of the Spanish Succession.

1702—French victory at Friedlingen.

1704—French defeat at Blenheim.

1706—French defeat at Ramillies. Marlborough reconquers Flanders. Eugene of Savoy defeats the French and conquers Turin.

1708—French defeat at Oudenaarde.

1709—French defeat at Malplaquet.

1711—Death of the Grand Dauphin, Louis XIV's son.

1712—French victory against the Allies at Denain. Death of the Duke of Burgundy, son of the Grand Dauphin.

1713—The Treaty of Utrecht followed by the treaties of Rastatt and Baden, brings to a close the War of the Spanish Succession.

1714—Death of the Duc de Berry, second son of the Grand Dauphin.

1715—September 1: Death of Louis XIV at Versailles.

The originals of the works reproduced in this volume can be found in the following collections: Chantilly, Musée Condé: pp. 5, 8, 9, 14, 15, 16. Florence, Uffizi: p. 63. Milan, Bertarelli Collection: pp. 6, 12, 16, 17, 18, 22, 26, 45, 59, 62, 63, 64, 67, 68, 69, 72, 73, 74. Paris, Louvre: pp. 4, 42, 43; Cabinet des dessins: 13, 26-27, 55; Bibliothèque Nationale, Cabinet des Estampes: pp. 4, 9, 10, 12, 13, 23, 26, 30, 34, 35, 37, 38, 39, 42, 49, 50, 58, 63, 64; Musée du Petit Palais: p. 18; Comédie Française, p. 65. Toulouse, Musée des Augustins: p. 13. Versailles, Bibliothèque: end papers, pp. 38, 39; Musée: pp. 5, 6-7, 10, 11, 19, 20-21, 23, 24-25, 29, 30-31, 32-33, 36, 37, 44-45, 46-47, 48, 49, 50, 51, 52-53, 54-55, 55, 57, 60-61, 66-67. Marquise d'Anglesey Collection: pp. 68-69. Bonjean-Brantôme Collection: p. 41. Photographic references: Alinari, p. 63. Paris, Bibliothèque Nationale: p. 9. Bulloz: pp. 37, 38. Connaissance des Arts, Photo Millet: p. 40. Draeger: pp. 40, 41. Giraudon: pp. 5, 12, 13, 14, 16, 18, 21, 24-25, 30-31, 34, 37, 42, 43, 52-53, 57, 65. E. Lessing, Magnum, p. 73. Saporetti: pp. 17, 18, 59, 62, 69, 72-73, 74. Scarnati: end papers, pp. 4, 5, 6-7, 8, 9, 10, 11, 13, 15, 19, 20-21, 23, 26-27, 29, 30, 32-33, 34, 35, 36, 38, 39, 42, 44-45, 46-47, 48, 49, 50, 51, 54-55, 58, 60-61, 64, 66-67. Weidenfeld and Nicholson: pp. 68-69, and the Mondadori Photographic Archives.